Sing With Coldplay!

This publication is not authorised for sale in the
United States of America and/or Canada

Wise Publications
part of The Music Sales Group
London/New York/Paris/Sydney/Copenhagen/Berlin/Madrid/Tokyo

Published by:
Wise Publications
8/9 Frith Street, London W1D 3JB, England.

Exclusive distributors:
Music Sales Limited
Distribution Centre, Newmarket Road,
Bury St Edmunds Suffolk IP33 3YB, England.
Music Sales Pty Limited
120 Rothschild Avenue, Rosebery, NSW 2018, Australia.

Order No. AM84682
ISBN 0-7119-2640-9
This book © Copyright 2003 by Wise Publications.

Unauthorised reproduction of any part of this publication by
any means including photocopying is an infringement of copyright.

Compiled by Lucy Holliday.
Music processed by Paul Ewers Music Design.
Vocals by Jo Edwards.
Guitars Arthur Dick.
Bass Paul Townsend.
Drums Brett Morgan.
Engineered by Jonas Persson.
Cover photograph courtesy of Rex Features.

Printed in the United Kingdom by Printwise (Haverhill) Limited, Haverhill, Suffolk.

www.musicsales.com

Clocks 4
Don't Panic 14
God Put A Smile Upon Your Face 9
In My Place 20
Trouble 16

Clocks

Words & Music by Guy Berryman, Jon Buckland,
Will Champion & Chris Martin

Guitar chords capo 1st fret

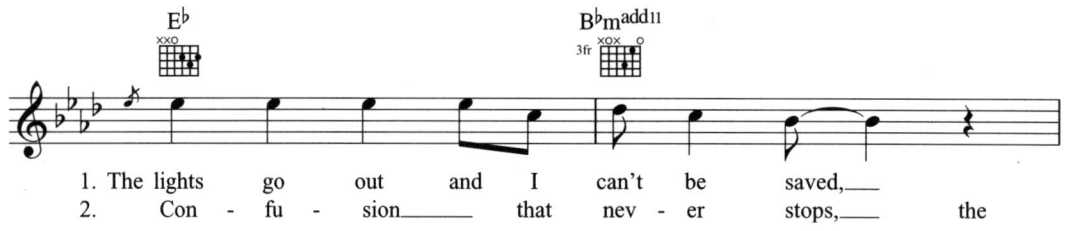

1. The lights go out and I can't be saved,
2. Con - fu - sion that never stops, the

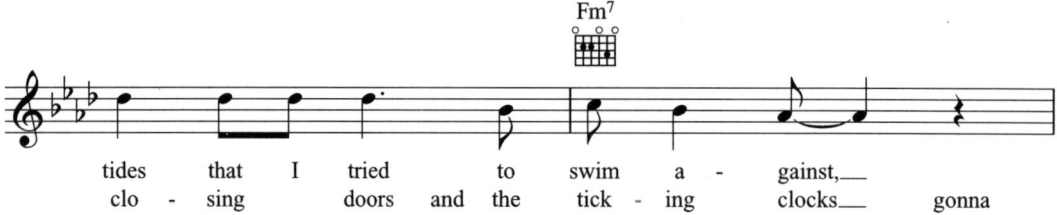

tides that I tried to swim a - gainst,
clo - sing doors and the tick - ing clocks gonna

© Copyright 2002 BMG Music Publishing Limited.
All Rights Reserved. International Copyright Secured.

E♭
B♭m7
Fm/A♭
You are.
G♭maj7
D♭
And no - thing else com - pares.
A♭6
G♭maj7
And no - - thing else
D♭
A♭6
G♭maj7
com - pares.
And no -
D♭
A♭6
- thing else com - pares.
G♭maj7
G♭maj9
G♭maj7
G♭maj9

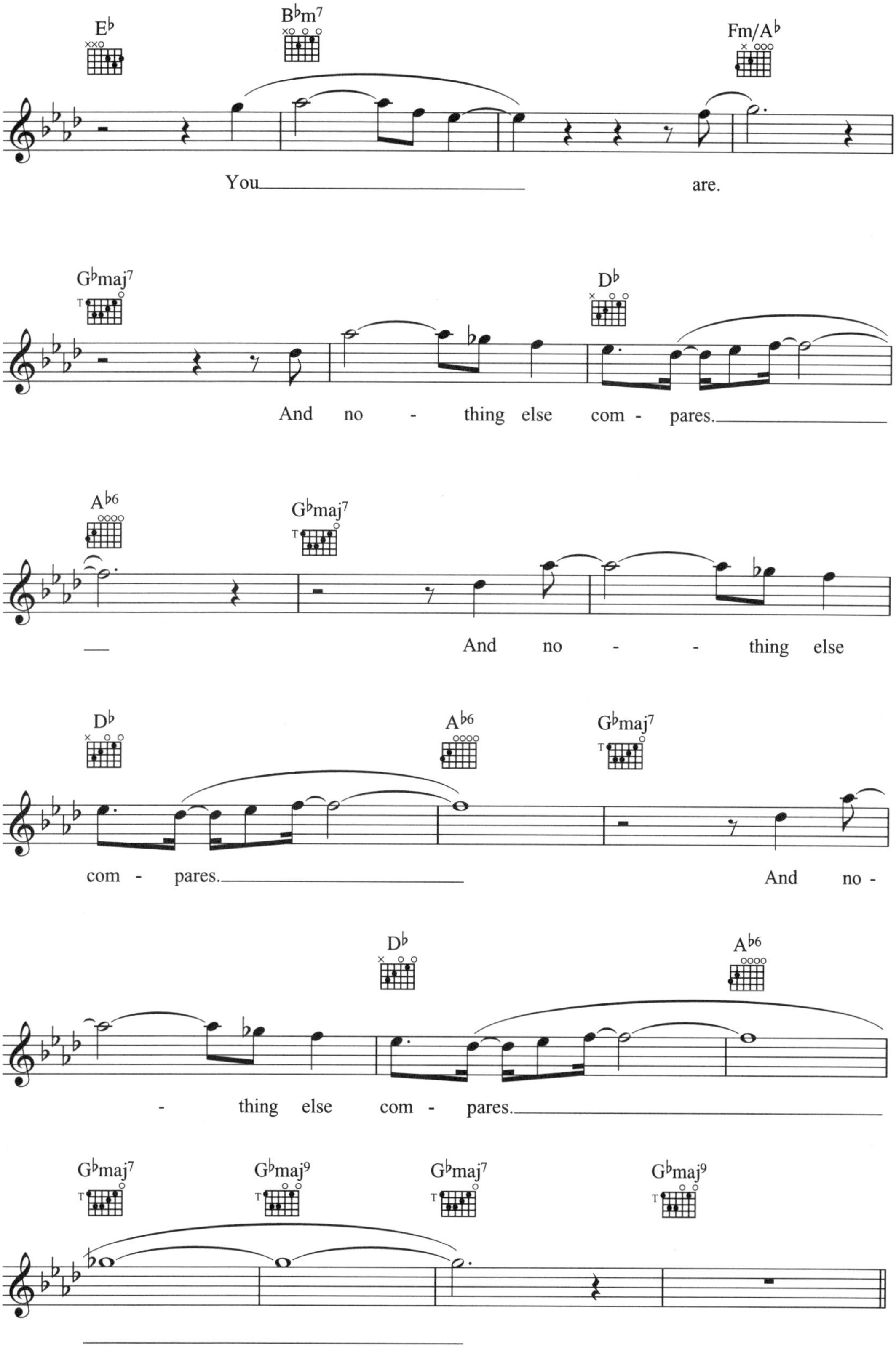

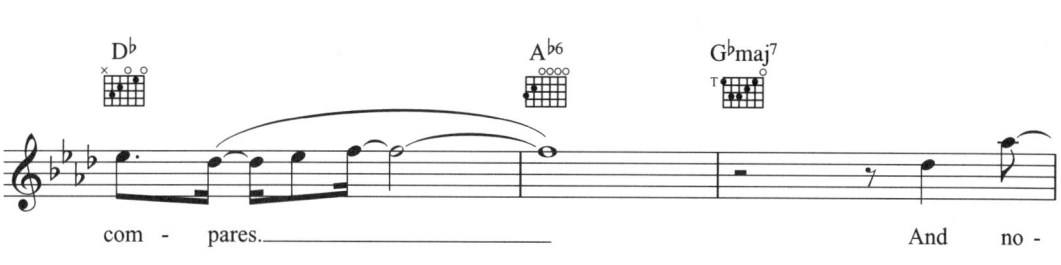

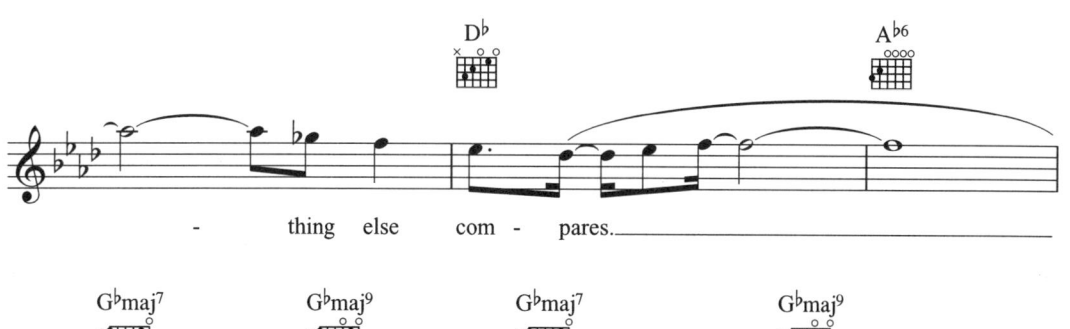

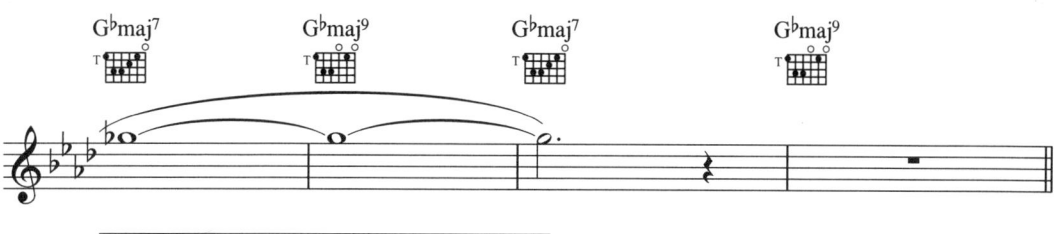

God Put A Smile Upon Your Face

Words & Music by Guy Berryman, Jon Buckland, Will Champion & Chris Martin

Tune guitar down one and a half tones

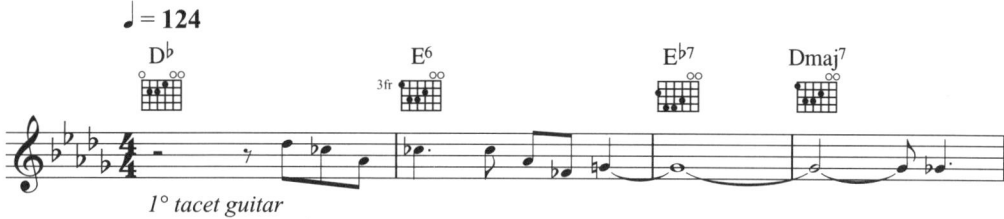

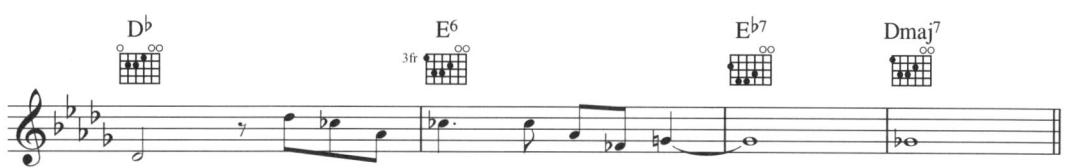

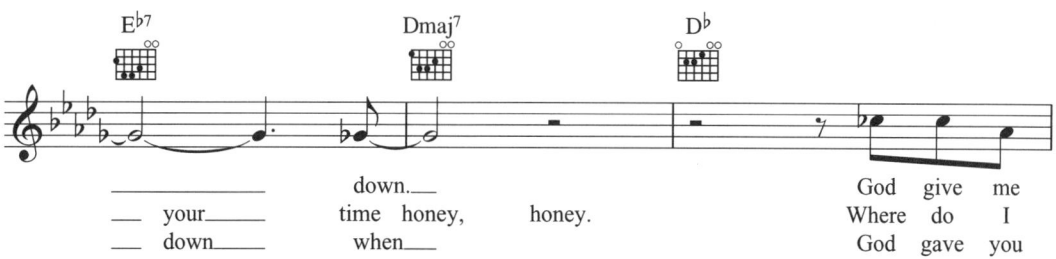

© Copyright 2002 BMG Music Publishing Limited.
All Rights Reserved. International Copyright Secured.

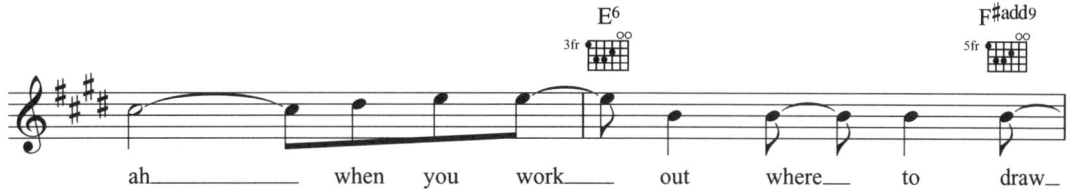
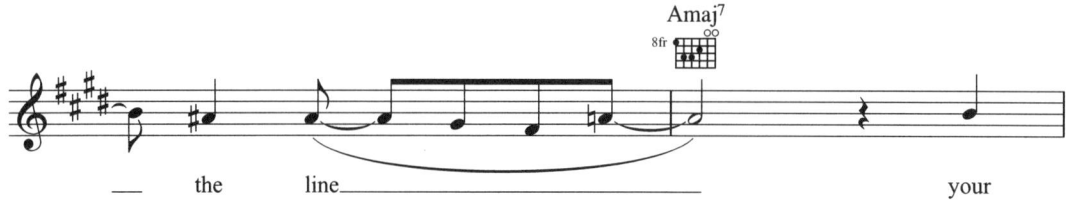
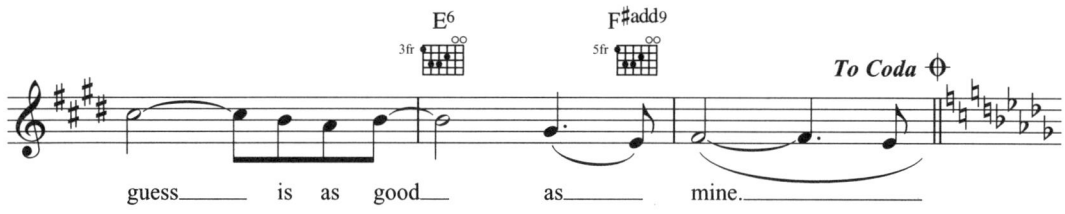

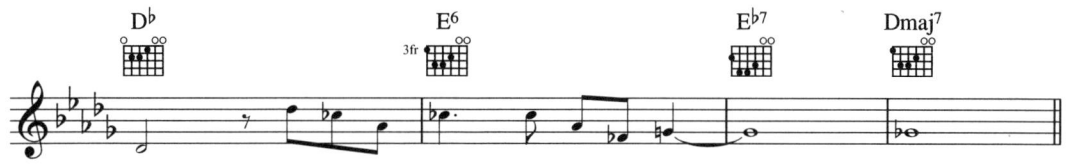
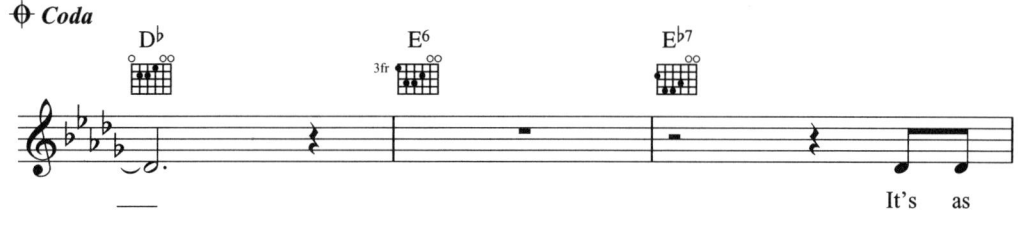

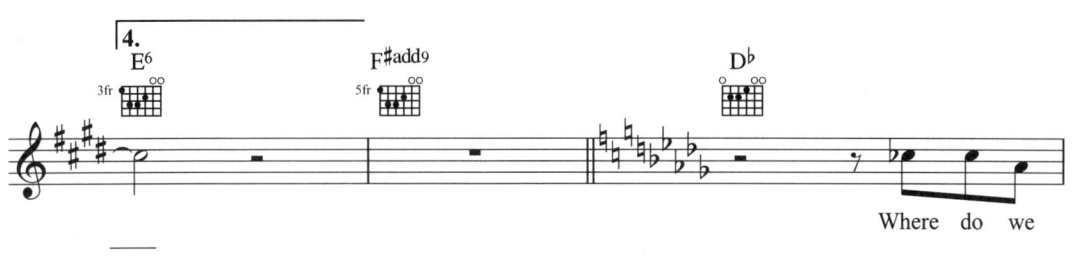
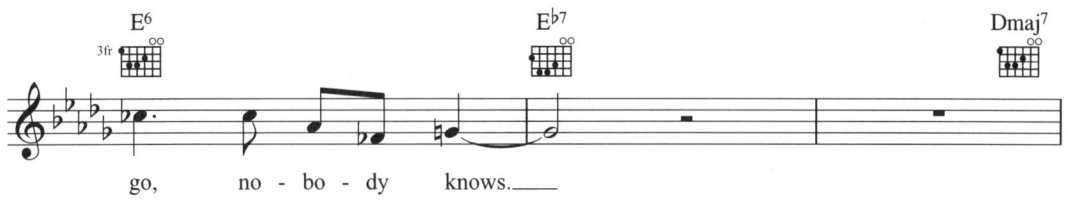

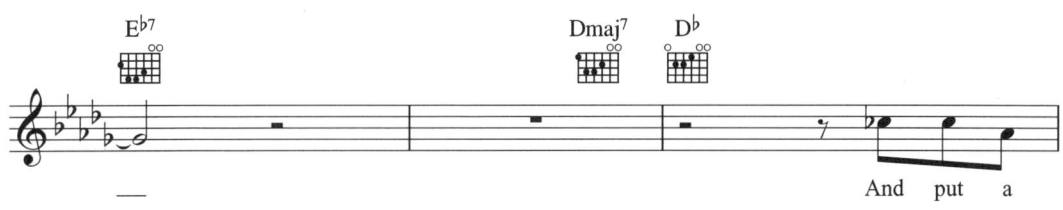
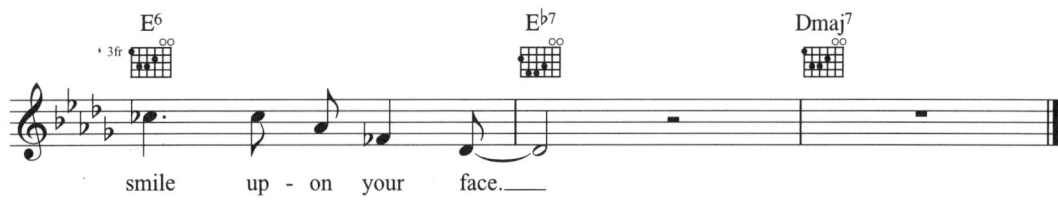

Don't Panic

Words & Music by Guy Berryman, Jon Buckland, Will Champion & Chris Martin

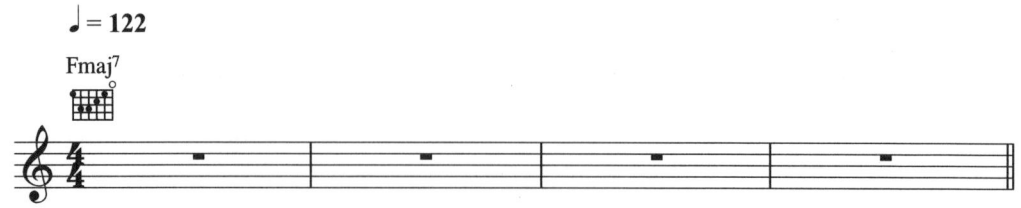

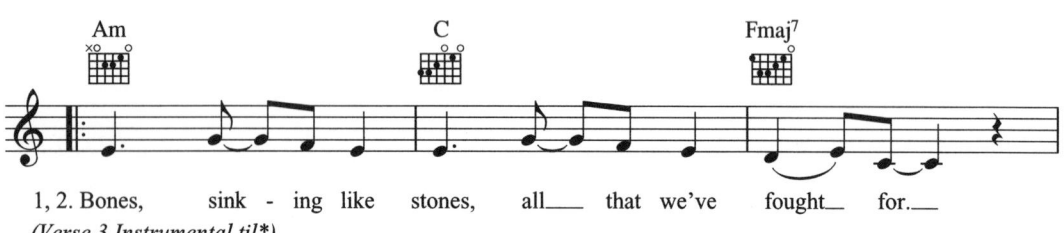

1, 2. Bones, sink - ing like stones, all that we've fought for.
(Verse 3 Instrumental til*)

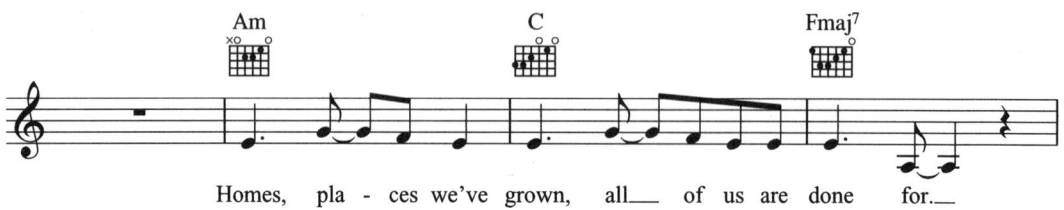

Homes, pla - ces we've grown, all of us are done for.

And we live in a beau - ti - ful world,
*

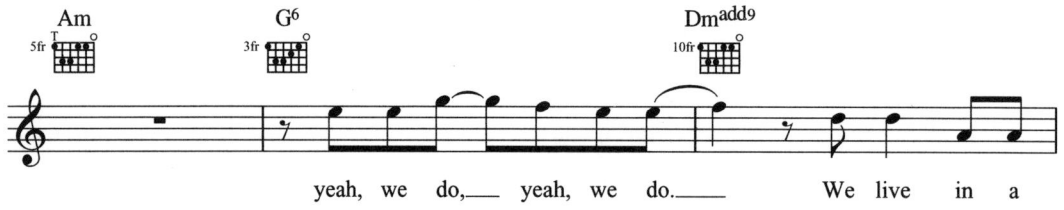

yeah, we do, yeah, we do. We live in a

© Copyright 2000 BMG Music Publishing Limited.
All Rights Reserved. International Copyright Secured.

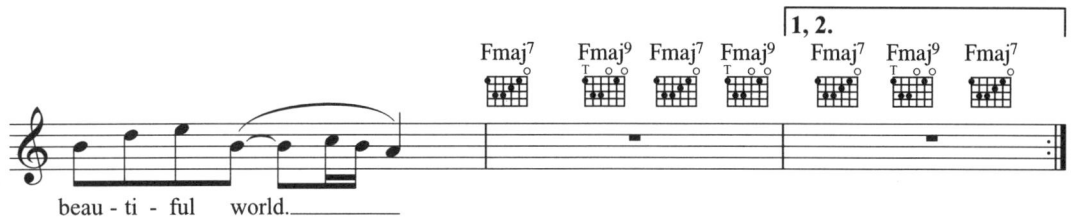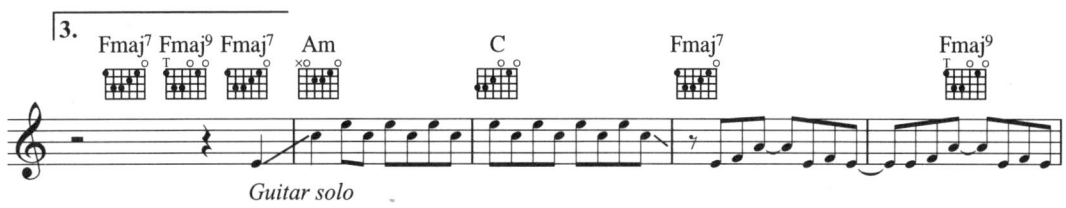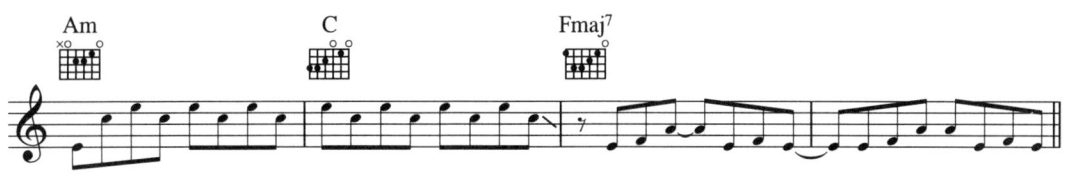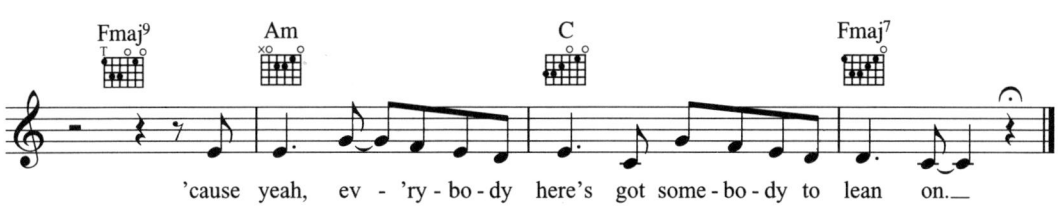

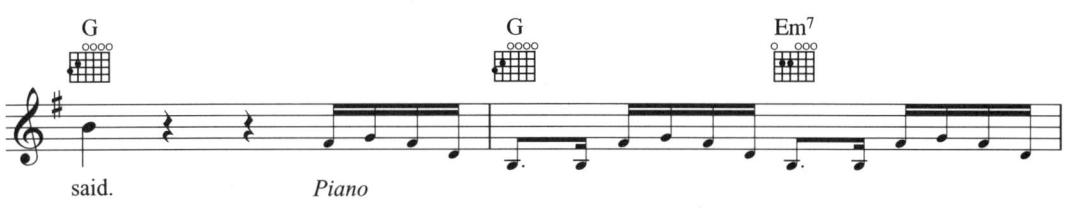
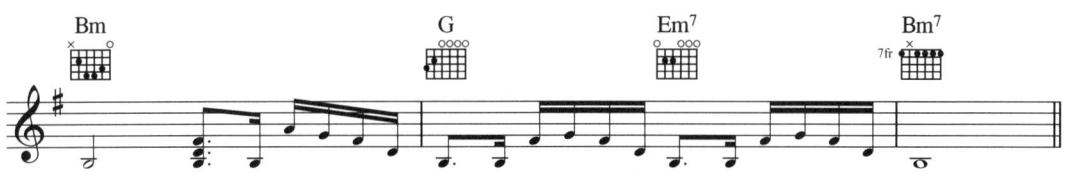
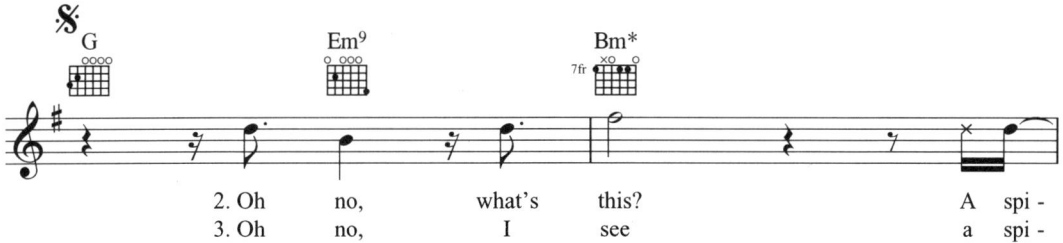

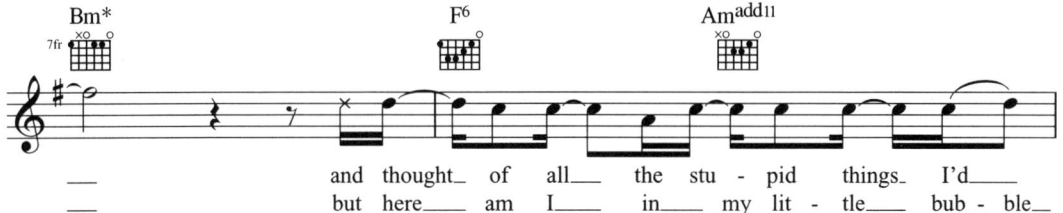
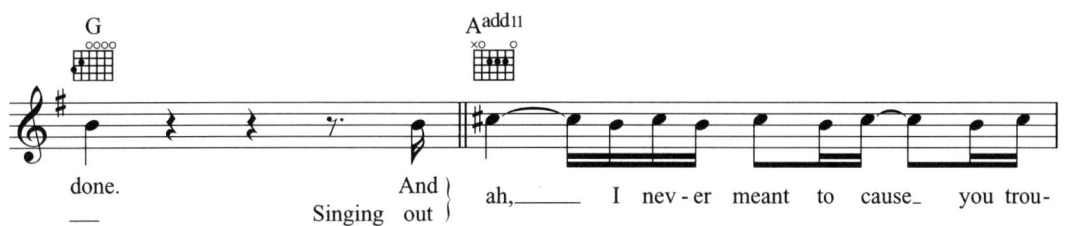

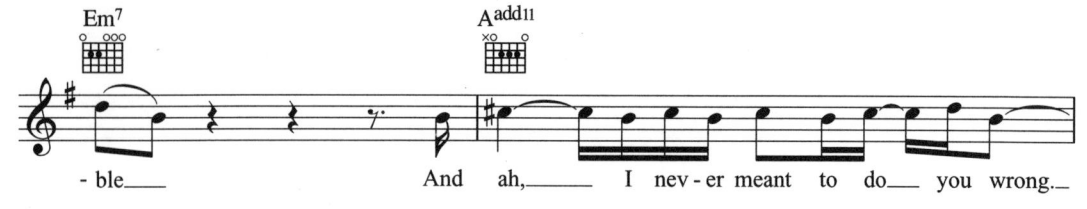
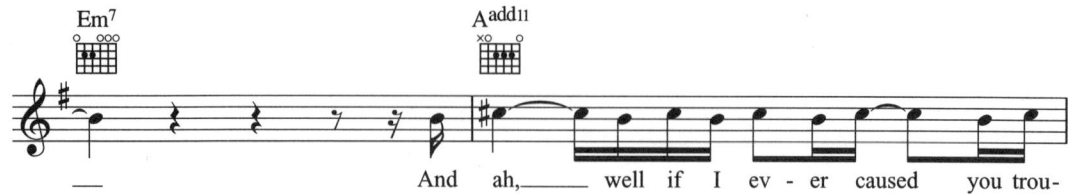

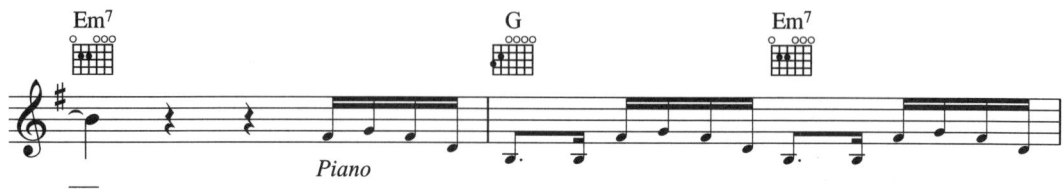
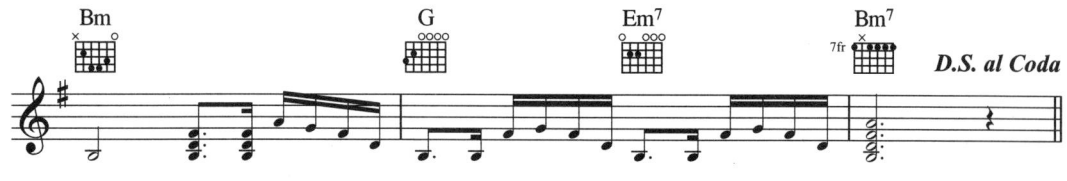
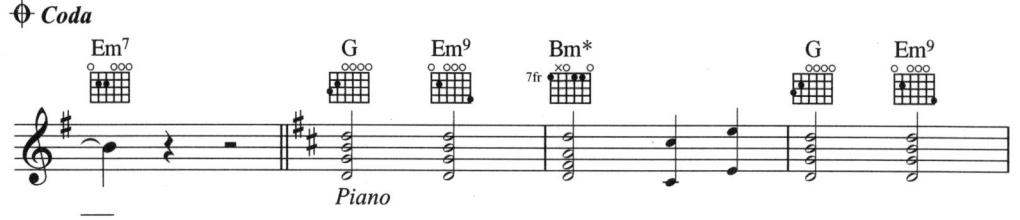

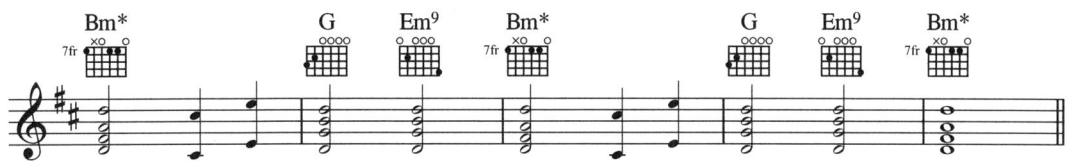
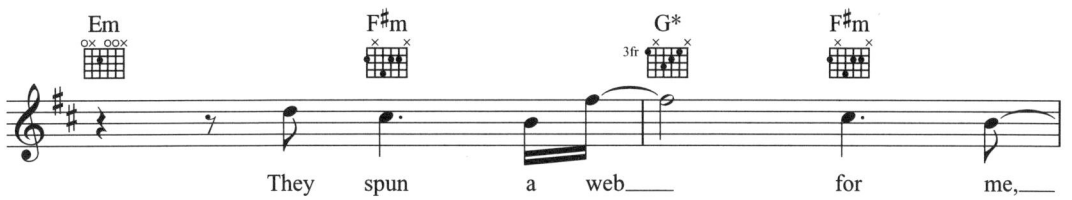
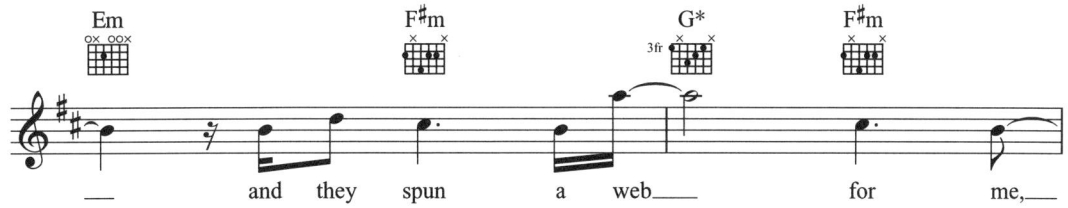
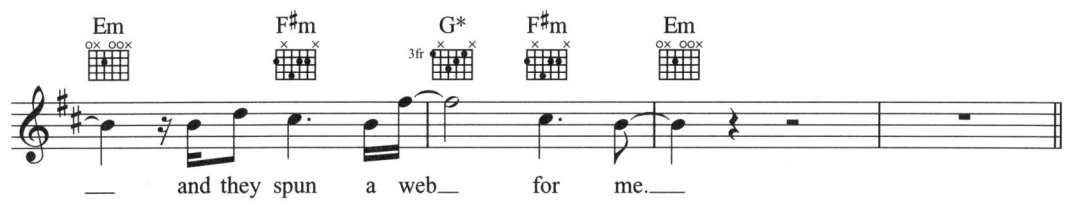
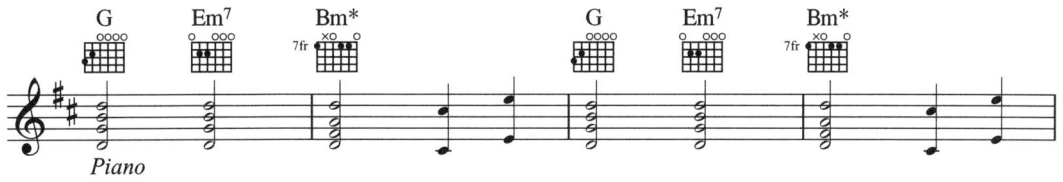

19

In My Place

Words & Music by Guy Berryman, Jon Buckland,
Will Champion & Chris Martin

Guitar chords capo 2nd fret

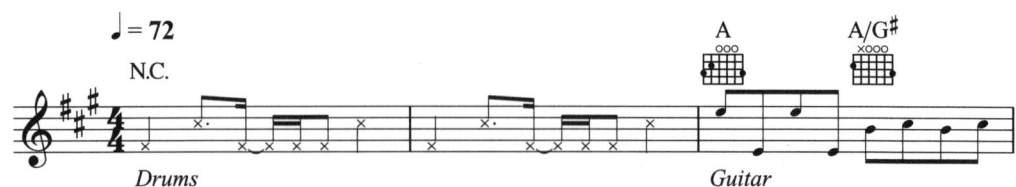
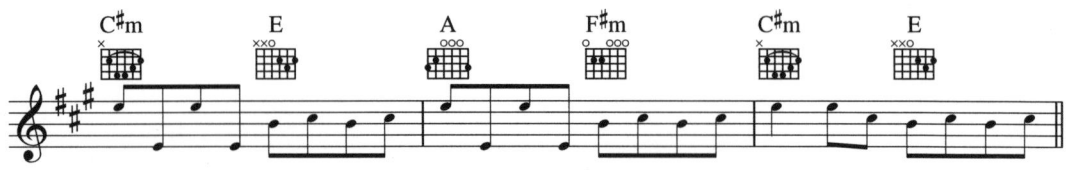
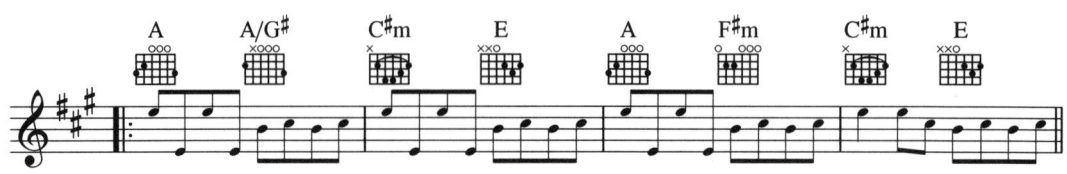

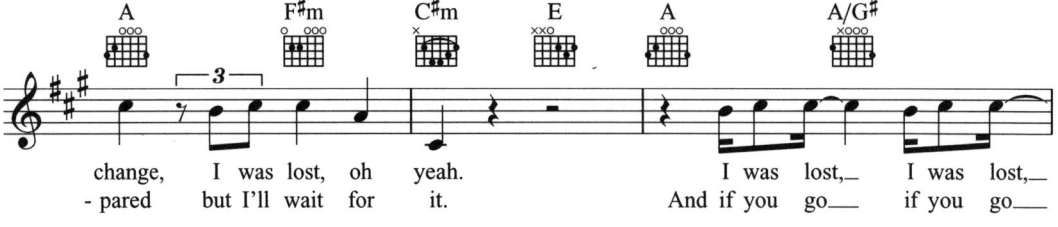

1. In my place, in my place were lines that I couldn't change, I was lost, oh yeah. I was lost, I was lost,
2. I was scared, I was scared, tired and under pre- pared but I'll wait for it. And if you go if you go

© Copyright 2002 BMG Music Publishing Limited.
All Rights Reserved. International Copyright Secured.

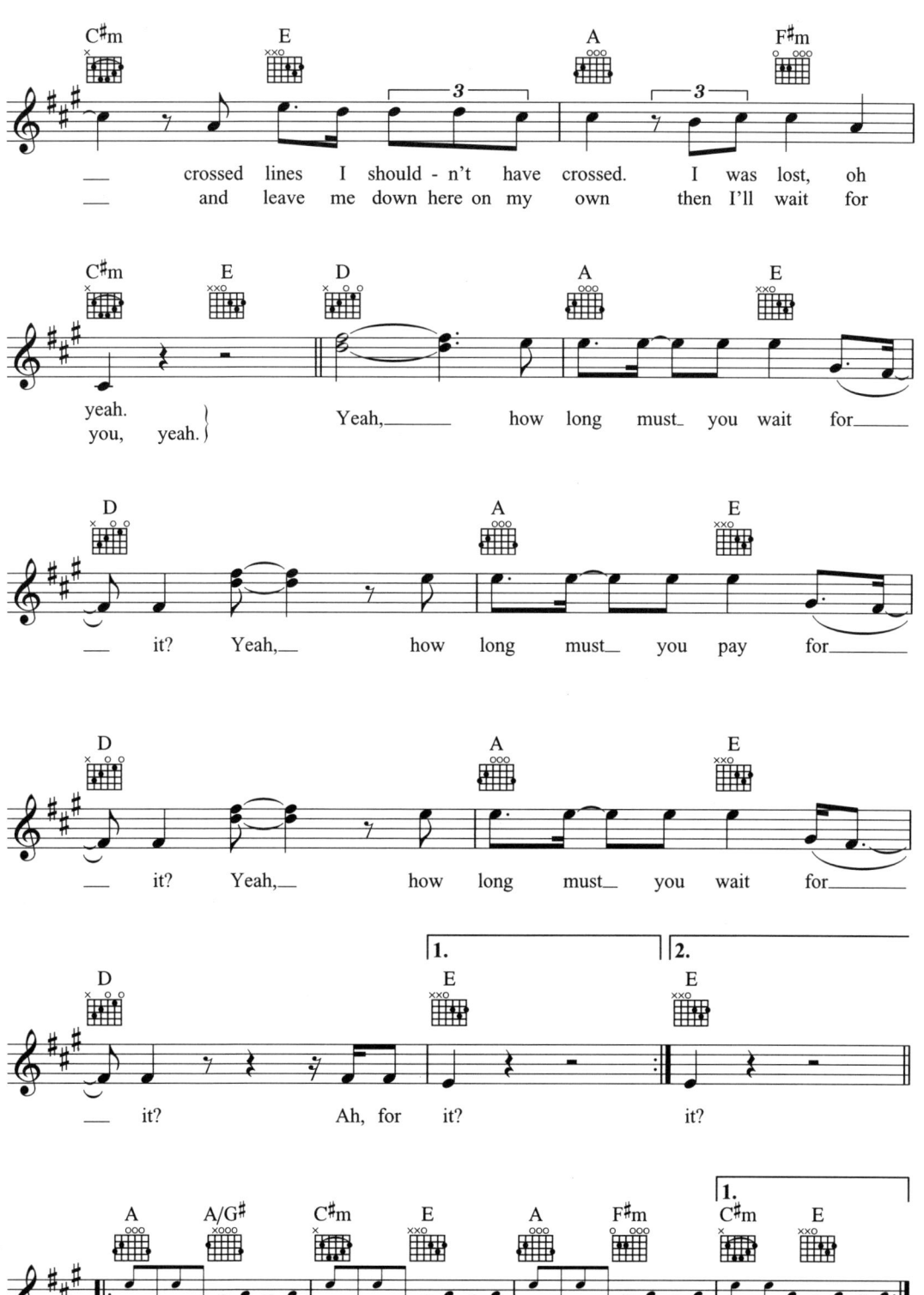

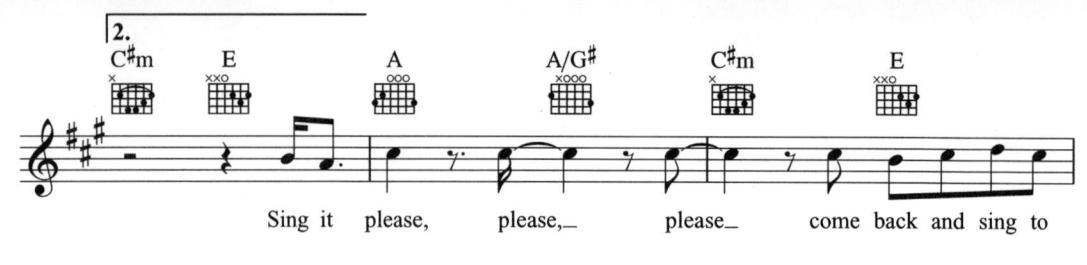
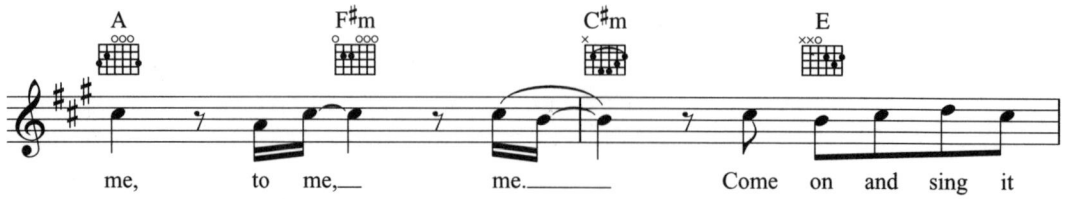
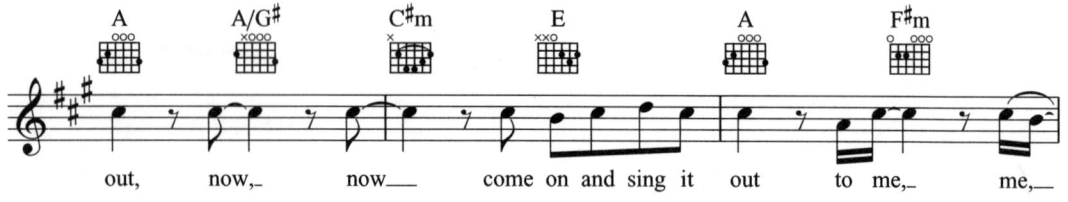
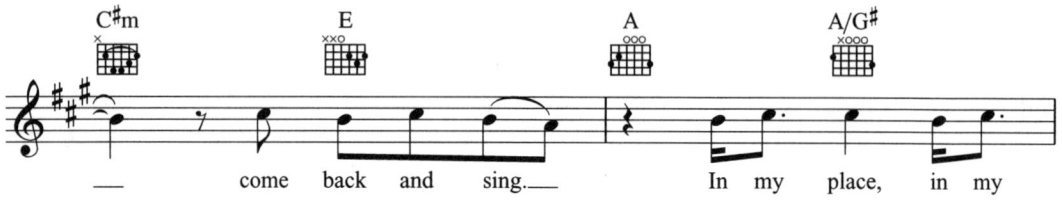
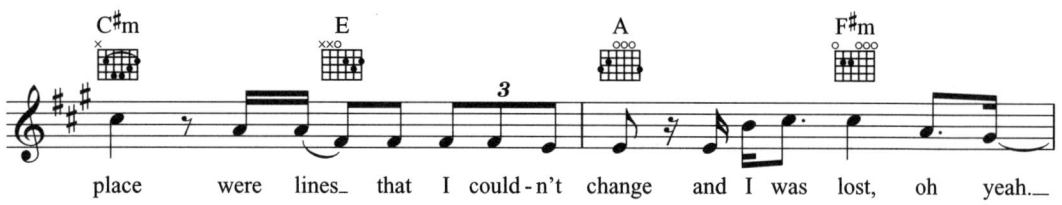
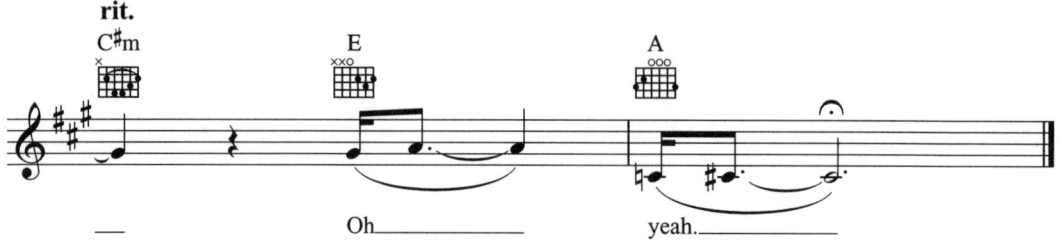

If you like this book you will also like these...

SING WITH ROBBIE
Sing along with five great singles by Robbie Williams, includes *Angels*, *Rock DJ* and *Supreme*.
AM969947

ROBBIE WILLIAMS SWING WHEN YOU'RE WINNING
Five great songs from this number one album, with great backing tracks to sing along with. Includes *Mack The Knife*, *Things* and *Ain't That A Kick In The Head*.
AM973929

SING MASSIVE HITS
Sing along with five massive anthems, including *Yellow* (Coldplay), *Why Does It Always Rain On Me* (Travis) and *Babylon* (David Gray).
AM971663

SING WITH ELVIS
Sing along with Elvis hits including, *Suspicious Minds*, *Blue Suede Shoes* and *A Little Less Conversation*.
AM975172

SING 16 CHART HITS
16 of the best chart hits of the past year for male and female singers, including songs by Blue, Daniel Bedingfield, Gareth Gates and Will Young.
AM976800

SING SOUL
Contains five great soul songs to sing along with, including *I Got You (I Feel Good)* (James Brown) and *Take Me To The River* (Al Green).
AM972180

SING 17 CLASSIC HITS
Sing along with 17 of the greatest pop songs ever! Includes *Wonderwall* (Oasis), *When You Say Nothing At All* (Ronan Keating), *Your Song* (Elton John) and *Somethin' Stupid* (Robbie Williams). For male and female singers.
AM976811

Available from all good music shops.
In case of difficulty, please contact:
Music Sales Limited
Newmarket Road, Bury St Edmunds, Suffolk, IP33 3YB.
www.musicsales.com

CD Track Listing

Full Demonstration Performances:

1 Clocks (Berryman/Buckland/Champion/Martin)
© Copyright BMG Music Publishing Limited.

2 God Put A Smile Upon Your Face (Berryman/Buckland/Champion/Martin)
© Copyright BMG Music Publishing Limited.

3 Don't Panic (Berryman/Buckland/Champion/Martin)
© Copyright BMG Music Publishing Limited.

4 Trouble (Berryman/Buckland/Champion/Martin)
© Copyright BMG Music Publishing Limited.

5 In My Place (Berryman/Buckland/Champion/Martin)
© Copyright BMG Music Publishing Limited.

Backing Tracks Only:

6 Clocks (Berryman/Buckland/Champion/Martin)
© Copyright BMG Music Publishing Limited.

7 God Put A Smile Upon Your Face (Berryman/Buckland/Champion/Martin)
© Copyright BMG Music Publishing Limited.

8 Don't Panic (Berryman/Buckland/Champion/Martin)
© Copyright BMG Music Publishing Limited.

9 Trouble (Berryman/Buckland/Champion/Martin)
© Copyright BMG Music Publishing Limited.

10 In My Place (Berryman/Buckland/Champion/Martin)
© Copyright BMG Music Publishing Limited.

MCPS All rights of the record producer and the owners of the works reproduced reserved. Copying, public performances and broadcasting of this recording is prohibited.

To remove your CD from the plastic sleeve, lift the small lip on the right to break the perforated flap. Replace the disc after use for convenient storage.